Convictions of the Heart

Poems by

John L. Holgerson

in case of emergency press

We are proud to acknowledge the Traditional Owners of country throughout Australia and to recognise their continuing connection to land, waters, and culture.

We pay our respects to their Elders past, present, and emerging.

We support recognition, reconciliation, and reparation.

in case of emergency press

http://www.icoe.com.au

Convictions of the Heart

John L. Holgerson

Acknowledgements

"Hydra, October 2010" and "Hydra, April 2019" first appeared in The Poetry Porch, 2021 edition

"The Thin Line," "One Night with the Sisters of Mercy at Christina's Taverna" and "Love Poem" first appeared in Page & Spine, the May 31, 2019 edition

"Finding Beauty" and "Broken Heart Repair" first appeared in Soaring Without Limits, June 1, 2019 edition

"Butterfly Heart" first appeared in Soaring Without Limits, April 5, 2017 edition

"Upon Seeing the Portrait of a Young Woman" first appeared in Visual Inverse, January 24, 2016 edition

"Crazy" appeared as MassPoetry's Poem of the Moment on September 28, 2015

"High White Stone House" first appeared in Page & Spine, the July 19, 2013 edition

"Panigiri" first appeared as "Evangelismós" and "Night in Rhodes" also first appeared in Concise Delight, Summer 2009

"Hydra, May 2006" first appeared as "Idra" in the Spring 2008 volume of Shadow Quill Poetry

"Tanka Triptych" first appeared as "Three Tanka" in Modern English Tanka, Volume 2, Number 2 (Winter 2007)

Published by In Case of Emergency Press 2021

Copyright 2021 © John L. Holgerson

All rights reserved. Without limiting the rights under copyright reserved above, no part of this publication may be reproduced, stored in or introduced into a database and retrieval system or transmitted in any form or any means (electronic, mechanical, photocopying, recording or otherwise) without the prior written permission of the owner of copyright.

ISBN 978-0-6485571-8-0

Table of contents

PROLOGUE	**1**
Things Remembered	3
HYDRA	**5**
Hydra, March 1970	7
Panigiri	8
Night in Rhodes	9
The Monastery	10
Hydra, May 2006	12
The Poet and the Painter	13
Blind Men Who Sail Yachts	14
Hydra, October 2010	15
Vantage Point	17
The Tender Thief	19
Hydra, April 2019	20
High White Stone House	22
One Night with the Sisters of Mercy at Christina's Taverna	23
Love Poem	25
Red Poppies Grow Wild Outside My Door	27
OTHER PLACES, OTHER PEOPLE	**29**
The Fence	31
The Sands of Cabo San Lucas	33
Those left behind alone	35
Tanka Triptych	36
Crazy	37
Gypsy Woman Dancing	38
Upon seeing the portrait of a young woman	39
The Thin Line	40
Loss of Appetite	41
Hypocrites	42
The Fourth Stinger Augury	43

Butterfly Heart	44
Broken Heart Repair	45
Finding Beauty	46
Postcards of America #1	47
Dublin	49
Sorrows of an Old Poet	50
Flowers Left in the Ground	51
To the Editors of Small Literary Journals	52
ABOUT THE AUTHOR	**57**

Don't write about ideas... Write about convictions of the heart

Leonard Cohen

For my parents
Jack and Rita

Prologue

Things Remembered
For JLH

Time, captured in a frayed tapestry
lining the frail cedar chest of memory,
boxed up by a year, a dying decade,
the turn of another nascent millennium.

For memories bind us all together.
The then and now married forever
as strong and as fragile as the
small and resolute red apple stem.

Hydra

There's not a day that goes by that I don't wake up and wish that I were there literally. I never wanted to be any other place in the world. It's just the place. It's just the place. It gets in your bones. I don't know how to describe it. It's just the place.
George Slater, American poet, trying to describe why he and so many other writers and artists are enchanted by the Greek island Hydra.

Whatever you saw, whatever you felt, whatever you held, was beautiful, and when you picked up a cup you knew by the way it fitted into your hand that it was the cup that you always had been looking for. And the table that you sat at, that was the table that you wanted to lean on, and the wine, that was ten cents a gallon, was the wine that you wanted to drink, the price you wanted to pay. The people that I bumped into, both the Greek and the foreigner, had the feeling of the people that I was meant to be with. This is the place where I was meant to be.
Leonard Cohen, Canadian poet, novelist, singer, songwriter describing living on Hydra in the early 1960s.

There are only two colors, blue and white, and the white is whitewashed every day, down to the cobblestones in the street. The houses are even more cubistically arranged than at Poros. Aesthetically it is perfect, the very epitome of that flawless anarchy which supersedes, because it includes and goes beyond, all the formal arrangements of the imagination.
Henry Miller, American novelist and artist describing his first in person view of Hydra.

Hydra, March 1970

Stone wall stitches
spiral up mountainsides
behind red-roofed rock houses
on which stray tom cats confide.

Chapels on hillsides
closed by time and desertion
cloaked in green moss shawls,
relics of the hoary pirates' religion.

Calls of donkeys are its engines
revved up by shrill whistles
from men with wooden whips.
Stone streets are its only trestles.

Above the tourist trap parasites,
where old men with whisk brooms
sweep up donkey dung drowned
in the scent of lilac and poppy fumes,

silent monks kneel down and gaze
upon a gray-hazed Peloponnese
thumbing well-worn worry beads
amid ancient arboreal sentries.

Panigiri

At sunset, lights lace the harbor.
Men and women stroll the waterfront
eating ice cream cones,
broken hearts hidden
among dissolving firework flashes.
Broken hearts elsewhere forgotten
on this night of laughter without tears.

Night in Rhodes

the sky melts
blue to indigo
you want to dip
your pen in it
to write what
antiquity
has left for you
to say

The Monastery

I've stood in some cold cathedrals
where sun-soaked stain glass windows
shower a spotlight of rainbows
on the Dove's empty nest resting
in ornate marble meadows.

Unconvinced by cathedrals
where the Dove was not at home,
I visited a saint's rotting relics
hidden from the hard-hearted Huns
in the sacred catacombs.

Here is my soul to tame.
Let it hear Your voice.
Let it hear You call me
by my only real name.

Carved on a torch lit wall
with a sprig of my sins in its beak,
the Dove kept watch over a virgin
tied to a tilted wooden cross set
afire on a stony mountain peak.

My pilgrimage incomplete,
I fled the bowels of martyrdom
to climb the steep mountain's side;
mud shackles round my ankles,
my filthy fingers bloodied numb.

Here is my soul to tame.
Let it hear Your voice.
Let it hear You call me
by my only real name.

On top, amid old pines, a monastery
stands forlorn in the virgin's honour.
A charcoal bearded monk bathed me,
frowned when I asked naively
why no man had ever won her.

Clothed in a monk's torn, tattered habit,
I see far above us the Dove as He hovers
in the sunset's lingering bright light,
the feathers of his world-weary wings
from the warm, narrow beds of His lovers.

Hydra, May 2006

Ancient
streets without cars
wind between white rock houses
on hills still stitched with stone walls
crumbling

where bright
red poppies grow
wild among the tall pines
while silent monastic monks pray
all night

'til dawn
when church bells ring
through the horseshoe harbour
where old men with donkeys sweep up
the dung

and wait
for the tourists
from ferries and long yachts
to pay for rides and marvel at
the view.

The Poet and the Painter

The poet and the painter
sit at old rickety wicker tables
outside the busy Buccaneer Bar.

With a wine glass in one hand,
she chooses her colours with care
from the fading harbour sunlight.

On a small, beer stained page,
the random words he writes
are always black on white.

Though he flexes his arthritic fingers
and she squints her scotopic vision,
their art is not once in doubt or debt.

The rising pain and annoyance
weave themselves into their work
wiping out any vestige of regret.

Blind Men Who Sail Yachts

Why are these men so blind
to the wistful women beside them?

They walk in their own world
talking money to be made,

gambles to be taken,
people to be played,

scores to be settled
before old memories fade.

Oblivious to the obeisant women
striding in silence next to them,

they do not see the tender looks
for the raggedy carefree children
cavorting on the crowded cobbled street,

the concern for the mud caked cats
begging by the barnacled fishing boats
docked in the busy horseshoe harbor,

or the trading of smiles with the man
who is watching from his seaside table
and who is writing this poem for them.

Hydra, October 2010

The fishing boats scuttle daily
in and out of the horseshoe harbour,
wooden and fibreglass crabs,
seeking a shoal of squid or sponge.
Tourist shops are bringing in their
postcard sentry stanchions and
wobbly wood tables with multi-color
tee shirts bearing the island's name.

Old timers stroke sweat from
bearded chins as they play
pinochle and backgammon for beer
and sausages in the old bars behind
the yacht-lined harbour front. The air
has become burdened by the thick
weight of an alien humidity. It clings
to the linings of the lungs like the
sudor-soaked clothes on our bodies.

And like the ancient rapacious
pirates buried unceremoniously in
unmarked graves, this bullying son
of global burning has stormed the
island's pine forests and seaboard
drying the groves to tinder while
pushing up the beaches' sandy skirts
so the Aegean can take by force areas
once beyond its greedy tidal grasp.

Some stores along the harbour front
will soon shut their double doors until
April when the poppies and tourists
will both bloom again and the winter winds
from Egypt and Israel will have blown this
bastard mugginess westward along with
some sudden, yet expected, Sahara sand.

Vantage Point

Where are you, darlin'?
I am waiting for you
on the high stone terrace
under the swaying umbrella,

bottle of sweet red wine,
pita bread and tzatziki
on the uneven wooden table.

Icarian sparrows soar sunward
only to plummet toward the sea.
Our candles, floating in boats
of olive oil, burn nearly to their nubs

as time brands the flesh with
brown spots like the rings
ever spiralling inside a tree.

I thought I saw you
flitting barefoot through the forest
of naked dying pines coming down
the mountain from the monastery.

Did you leave those ancient monks
a psalm beneath their pristine pillows?
A hallelujah to holler toward Kamini?

There is a young woman strolling
across the sunny harbour front.
A true cambry, every man's dream.

Long straight black hair draped
over dark sun-kissed shoulders;
her gypsy hands tucked into the
pockets of a swirling scarlet skirt.

A young man zigzags through
the tourists toward her. He holds a
small bouquet of red and yellow
lilies; his imperfect offering. Clean shaven,

denim shirt open at the collar, paint spots
polka dot his wrinkled white pants.
Anticipation pools like rain in his eyes.

The loud rasp of the rusty door hinge
tells me you are here. Come then,
sit close to me in the fading twilight.

From this granted vantage point
of gods, let us raise our glasses,
toast those oppressed by beauty,
and watch what happens next.

The Tender Thief

I remember what you
whispered in my ear the
morning when you left:

"I have your heart. You
can keep your soul for
I won't leave a man bereft

of his dizzy dreams
or his crazy schemes
or what was slyly said

during tender scenes
played out beneath
the covers of his bed."

Hydra, April 2019
for Leonard Cohen (1934-2016)

I stood outside
your old home today
as I've done in years past.
Tangled ivy vines from the roof
terrace stretched down the wall
toward me, a thin green leafy rope,
inviting me to grab its strands with
both hands and pull myself up.

If I was a younger man perhaps;
but my wall-scaling days ceased long ago.
Instead, I looked for the wire and the bird.
I saw the former: a tightrope, taut and thin,
pole-tied between red-roofed white houses.
There was no sparrow, but I'm still here
listening for what cannot be heard.
I put my hand on the wall of your house

hoping the lingering remnant of a once
strummed guitar riff or the clickety-clack
of your old, olive green Olivetti would
course through my fingertips, run the
maze of jagged lines on my smooth palm,
up my willing arm to the area of the brain,
or whatever part of the soul, sends messages
to the Muse assigned to a scribbler of verse.

But it doesn't work that way does it, Leonard?

That singular Muse here for you then isn't mine.
Although I'd like to think they may be sisters
or, more likely, cousins once or twice removed.
At Douskos Taverna, I dined on fresh xiphias
under the huge old pine tree where, once
upon a time before fame and fortune fell
upon you, you sat, sang and played guitar
for Marianna and all your Hydriot friends.

I'll come by tomorrow. You never know,
someone or something may be at home.

High White Stone House

I don't think of you much
in this high white stone house
with silence an unseen shade
drawn on each unshuttered window.

Outside, the buzz of flies on poppies
as loud as saws on redwood.
The clop of hooves on carved rock stairs
as empty as the chairs in the living room.

No sound replicates your laughter
burning moussaka in the kitchenette
or your violin serenading the gypsies
on the boats in the horseshoe harbor.

The creak of the door
creeps across these walls.
The breath of the wind stutters.

You standing on the terrace
naked from the back,
a ghost who sometimes mutters.

When shutters close at day's end,
a hungry dark slides over me
inside this high white stone house
this hollow unending echo of you.

One Night with the Sisters of Mercy at Christina's Taverna
for K, R & V

Three Ivy League women
invited me to sit at their table
one random night at this taverna.

They were in their twenties.
Me, let's just say for the record,
I once passed through that decade.

I talked American politics
with K who, born in Nova Scotia,
cannot cast a vote in America.

I spoke about the vicissitudes
of love with V and how they can
lead to some unnecessary tattoos.

I discussed the sad state
of a certain writer's web site
with R as she built one for the taverna.

I drank their red, red wine,
listened to their circumspect words,
was humbled by their warm welcome.

Like a thirsty flower with a spring rain,
I took in their youth and beauty
and felt the weary weight of age wane.

The enticements of Byron
the yearnings of Yeats
the supplications of Cohen

toward young women in their work
became much clearer to me as
late night stole the early evening from us.

I thank the Sisters of Mercy for this poem
and their unconditional kindness to the elderly
on the eve of their departure from Idhra.

There are so many women
like them for whom I have not
written a poem nor ever will.

Love Poem

Someday I will leave you
and not come back. I hear
you laughing from deep
within the stones and rocks
at the core of your old heart.

You give more than you get.
At least that's the case with me.
But I am drawn to you
like the rapt suicidal moth
to the forever flirting flame

even if you never give me
another word. It isn't the
exiled thrum of rubber tires
or the sunsets that set ablaze
the entire Peloponnesian coast.

I am here with you
for the same reasons
I tell anyone who asks:
You heal my heart
and cure my soul.

But someday I will leave
you and not ever return.
I already know that you

will not miss me or even
note that I am absent.

For you only give to me
and never deign to ask
for anything from me.
You cannot miss what
you have never received.

So now I offer you this poem
in humble gratitude for all
the lines you've given to me
including those genuflecting
for you on this trembling page.

Red Poppies Grow Wild Outside My Door

I've flown in packed airplanes,
sailed across rough oceans blue,
ridden on noisy subway trains,
just to find my way back to you.

White houses with red slate roofs
near little shops and old pirate bars
join family tavernas and small churches
on this Greek island devoid of cars.

Braying donkeys and ritzy yachts,
fishing boats and dirty scows
all harbour-tied with different knots
by tired sailors and monks with cowls.

I live in a house high above the harbour,
red poppies grow wild outside my door.
The sun shines through large windows
and sweeps away shadows on the floor.

Village lights wink on slowly one by one
when the sun, moon and stars all engage.
Candle stubs float on corks in olive oil.
My pencil rests on a waiting white page.

I've flown in packed airplanes,
sailed across rough oceans blue,
ridden on noisy subway trains,
just to find my way back to you.

Other Places, Other People

One needs a place in which to play and one must play with language to engage a place at all in poetry... I'm not much interested in unpopulated landscapes
    from an interview with Samizdat magazine, Spring 2002

Still, the poet transcribed secret words directly in his poems
                                   from "Francophiles, 1958"

John Matthias, American poet, novelist, essayist

The Fence

Maria came to the small hill at sunset.
She crawled to the top on her stomach,
her elbows digging in the dirt like pistons.
She carried her father's small strapless
black binoculars in her right hand.

Making sure the waning sun was at her back
so there would be no gleam off the lenses,
she raised them to her eyes and saw the fence.
It was a soccer field away. Scanning it slowly,
she found the board with the Z-like split in it.

Night, her accomplice, joined her on the hill.
Maria descended in a crouch to the Big River.
The half moon glint guided her to its bank.
The Big River, now parched and shallow
from the long, hot drought, invited her.

The warm brown water climbed skinny legs
to narrow hips, then receded resentfully.
Maria slithered along the marshy ground.
At the fence, she yanked down on the Z board.
It cracked open and a yawning hole appeared.

She could smell the fertility and richness
of the soil. It hung like drying laundry in
the night air. *American Freedom*, she thought.
She scurried through the hole, snapped the
broken board into place, stood and stretched.

The welcome cheer of cicadas was deafening.
Looking up, she watched swift storm clouds
eat the last remnants of the handicapped moon.
Full dark enveloped her. Warm rain drops kissed
her face and cruised the wide contour of her smile.

The Sands of Cabo San Lucas
For ALD (1964-2019)

She always told me that the
beach sand at Cabo San Lucas
was like small flakes of gold
and that sunsets were sparklers
when she watched them lying on
a chaise lounge through the sand
she'd kidnapped between her toes.

She even sent me a photograph
of bare legs and bare feet (she
claimed to be hers) facing a
blazing sun diving into the ocean.
On its back, a note imploring me
to look at that sun through her toes
but I could never see what she saw.

There were other things she told me.
Some made me laugh until I cried;
some broke my heart so I just cried.
I gave her some of my poems to read.
Some made her laugh until she cried;
some broke her heart so she just cried.
(Did I thank her for reading my poems?)

Wrecked by this unforeseen sandbar
of sad news, I rummaged through a box

with a wind up sheep and a brown pen
set she had given me and found the
photograph of very pale bare legs and
bare feet and saw the sunset glowing,
a bright sparkler, between her toes.

Those left behind alone
a poem from the 2020 pandemic

you think you know the answer
you think you found the way
but the path keeps disappearing
with the break of dawn each day.

the quiet of each long night
the slow ticking of the clock
trick you into thinking you can
see the direction you should walk.

the morning light so bright
the warm sun in the afternoon
the sound of little children laughing
confuse night's casting of the rune.

the absence of their voice
the faint scent of their perfume
fight some crazy twisted battles
in the dark corners of every room.

you think you know the answer
you think you found the way
but the path keeps disappearing
in the echo of things they used to say.

Tanka Triptych

the absence of you
a shawl across my shoulders
drawn tighter by
the stillness of trees
the silence of birds

watching the moon float
amid cruising charcoal clouds
an ashen buoy
on an onyx ocean
I thought of you tonight

the old dog lies down
headstone shade blankets him
he waits as before
head on the ground dreaming
in smell of earth, scent of home

Crazy

with an apology to H.D. Thoreau

Crazy is the detergent
scrubbing the scum
of quiet desperation
from the wheels of destiny.

Crazy is the roulette ball
coming to rest
on your odd number
when all your friends are even.

Crazy is the last chance
to forego the normalcy
no one can define
but everyone claims to have

and to dance
naked and alone
on ancient marble stairs
unafraid of history,

yours or theirs,
as cold stone numbs
blisters burning
the soles of your gypsy feet.

Gypsy Woman Dancing

She came into the noisy barroom
with Romani guitar riffs in the air.
Her green eyes flashing subtle heat,
bare shoulders shawled by black hair.

She swirled her long red tiered skirt
as the mystic music ebbed and flowed.
I would not have traded that moment
for Nizam's jewels or pirate gold.

Watching her twirl slowly toward me,
mesmerized by the sound of the zills,
I could not move and, barely breathing,
surrendered the remnants of my will.

Swaying her hips, she brought her hand
to my face and stroked my burning cheek.
Then smiled and danced away from one
more prisoner in a long unbroken streak.

Upon seeing the portrait of a young woman

Who are you
to hold me here
with an over-the-shoulder glance
in this stylish tabernacle
of sketched and painted visions
where art asks poetry to dance?

When your winter comes
and the crows of time tramp
'round the corners of your eyes,
this face will be the same,
youth's presumed immortality
affirmed and age itself disguised.

And when the snow is deep
and you are warm before the fire,
rapt by love poems in some old book,
remember the hearts of gold
a silent beauty stole
with a single mesmeric look.

I was not beguiled
by how brush, oil and canvas wed
'til I saw your face by chance;
who are you
to hold me here
with this over-the-shoulder glance?

The Thin Line
for W. Somerset Maugham

He went to the cheap restaurant
and watched her work every day.
He ordered tea and a cake for
which he knew he could pay.

He thought she danced her way
between the crowded tables.
She became that princess who
lives in so many well-told fables.

He flirted. She flirted. All the time
with other men when he wasn't there.
As long as she let him take her out
and spend the night, he didn't care.

His want for her may have been
love first or maybe naked desire.
Being with her, having her for himself
became his passion, his driving fire.

He wanted to admit his suffocating
need for her. A penitent at confession.
He never saw the thin line that exists
between lust and love and obsession.

Loss of Appetite

I saw you standing with
your suitcase by the door.
The shattered glass of milk
a Rorschach on the floor.

Your smile said "So sorry."
Your eyes were full of hurt.
You left the kitchen with
the smell of something burnt.

I thought of going after
you striding down the street.
But pride was an anchor
saying "You ain't the cheat."

So I slumped on a chair.
There was food on the table.
I decided I would eat
as soon as I was able.

It's been quite a while now.
I've spent this time alone.
The food's still on the table
and I'm just skin and bone.

Hypocrites

I never wanted your body
the way the others did.
It seemed so cheap, so tawdry,
pornographic, sordid.

I don't see you very often
the way the others do,
swimming with the dolphins,
enjoying your little coup.

But that's alright, it's not uncouth
the way the others speak.
The bitter taste of truth
peels the tongue off my cheek.

The Fourth Stinger Augury

Some time ago,
when we were not lovers,
you left me as though we were.
And now, all these years later,
you want to come back to me.

Is this what you meant
that bygone night at Bill's Bar
when, after your fourth Stinger,
you told me in a mellow murmur,
"Irony isn't just a literary device?"

Butterfly Heart

Her heart is a battered butterfly
floating from one inconstant lover to another,
looking for compassion and honesty
while keeping its own undercover.

Anonymous she lets it flit time away
in a garden of chat rooms she grows online;
talking about sad and broken moments,
some quite profane, some quite divine.

And in her nights of solitude,
quiet but for some soft sighing,
her heart finds solace in the simple fact
no one can hear a butterfly crying.

Broken Heart Repair

In order to protect her fickle heart
from being stolen and broken again
by another callous but seductive liar,

she cauterized the caustic cracks with gin,
Gorilla Glued the pieces, and stitched them
very carefully with razor-sharp barbed wire.

Finding Beauty

If you study
the blue and gold wings
of a cavalier butterfly cruising
amid a field of willing wildflowers
their pliant petals opening at its approach,

if you visit
the Mecca of your restless dreams
where penitent pine trees climb
ancient monastic mountainsides
and the blue sea below is clear and pure,

if you gaze upon
the face and form of your lover
mesmerized by their fine symmetries
lying so close to your timid touch
covered only by early morning light,

do you think
you have found the elusive Beauty
coveted by our ill-fated forefathers,
the Beauty we ourselves cannot define
within the poverty of our unworthy vocabulary?

Come closer. Allow me
to whisper in the tunnel of your ear
the soft and harsh eternal echo
of flawed flesh and stained soul:
this search never ends.

Postcards of America #1

In the cities,
the walking wounded
of many unseen wars,
domestic and foreign

battlefields of
desert sands, kitchen
tables, intervention
rooms, court rooms,

stumble in the streets.

Their stories written in
rheumy eyes, drunken
tattoos, sticker-stained
stolen shopping carts.

In the farmlands,
the walking wounded
of the same unseen wars,
domestic and foreign

battlefields of
desert sands, kitchen
tables, foreclosed
mortgages, muddy
unploughed lands,

stumble in the swards.

Their stories written with
calloused hands and feet,
ancient, rusted tractors,
broken politicians' promises.

America, America,
land of opportunity
for its fortunate sons
and daughters yet unborn.

Dublin

The books in the Trinity Library age in silence.
Pages turn yellow like late autumn leaves.
Bindings, loose and old bone brittle, crack
and shatter in the stacks without a single sound.

The worn working men in the glass-clacking pubs
argue politics hard but speak soft of broken hearts.
They'll buy you a pint at the stabscotch scarred bar
and not expect you to pony up for the next round.

Young women smile at old men as they pass
on the crowded, senescent cobblestone streets.
In the air, the music of guitar and fiddle criss-cross,
and the old men grin recalling what has been lost.

The meadows are replete with rainbow wildflowers.
Lough Tay is deep blue, calm and snow crystal cold.
But Nature has repainted the green of the North's grass
where the blood of neighbours reddened the ground.

Yet young women smile at old men as they pass
on the crowded, senescent cobblestone streets.
The Troubles skulks in the shadows, undying ghost,
and the old men grimace recalling all who've been lost.

And the books in Trinity Library age in silence.
Pages turn yellow like late autumn leaves.
Bindings, loose and old bone brittle, crack
and shatter in the stacks without a single sound.

Sorrows of an Old Poet

I gave a poem to a girl
while riding on a train.
She glanced at it, gave
it back and told me to refrain

from writing about young
women's beauty like a swain.
"It's unseemly 'cause you're
old and long out of the game."

"But what about Neruda
and Yeats?" I exclaimed.
"You're not either of them,"
she said with great disdain.

Then I gave a poem to a girl
riding on a different train.
She read it with close scrutiny
thanking me with loud acclaim.

"You don't think it's unseemly
'cause I'm old and out of the game?"
"No. What about Neruda
and Yeats?" she exclaimed.

I wanted to talk with her further
but the train came to North and Main.
She got off with a smile and blew
a kiss before I could learn her name.

Flowers Left in the Ground

The poems seeded
in the heart's core
overwatered with
torrid yet innocent

tears like those shed for
the loss of a favourite toy
or for a cruel slight
unjust and undeserved

or for the callous lover
who leaves before first light.
Their roots maze-entwined
in the hapless heart's dim

and dank corners where
grief lets regret grow wild
amid the dense, bitter weeds
of obdurate anger and revenge

lurking just outside the vast
warm, radiant enclaves where
blithe joy and cheer reside and
abiding hope and doubt collide.

To the Editors of Small Literary Journals

This is just a note
to let you know
that, in the end,
it doesn't matter which
of us unknown poets
you choose to publish;

whether our poems
are "right for your
publication" or fit
whatever "the vision"
of it may be in your
often narrow viewpoints.

None of us will gain
literary or spiritual
immortality by being
the ones chosen to appear
in the pages of your print
journals or online ezines.

This humbling and
overdue realization
comes to me after
having written lines
for so many decades
in my own or copied styles

for the partisans oppressed
by the powers of beauty
and passion. Or, as another
poet said, for "the few who
forgive what you do and the
fewer who don't even care."

I've had poems published
in the print and cyberspace
worlds of today's poetry and,
make no mistake, much of it
was luck. Oh, some small
artistic skill was no doubt
collaterally involved.
Some ability to tell a story
that my readers recognized;
that hit a universal note in
the different arpeggios
of their ordinary daily lives.

And while I received more
letters of acceptance than
rejection from discerning,
perceptive editors like you
(for which I remain grateful),
I realize now what I

naively ignored before:
None of it will gain me

immortality in the literary
art of poetry or in the
practical art of salvation
of the soul which we

all are in dire need of.
Yet I still continue to write
lines only some few will
peruse and hope that none
of you, dear Editors, will
be my poems' last reader.

About the author

John L. Holgerson is the author of two books of poetry, *Unnecessary Tattoo and Other Stains on a Stainless Steel Heart* (Finishing Line Press 2016) and *Broken Borders* (Wasteland Press 2012). He has published poems in small literary journals, both in print (*Modern English Tanka; Shadow Quill Poetry; Popt Art* among others) and online (*Page & Spine; Vincent van Gogh Gallery; MassPoetry; The Poetry Porch* among others). He has been a featured poet at poetry venues in southeastern Massachusetts (*Poetry: The Art of Words; Calliope; Arts & Humanity* among others) and the greater Boston area (*Chapter and Verse*). He is the host of *For the Love of Words*, a monthly program on Easton (MA) Cable Access Television showcasing regional and local poets and musicians. He produced, moderated and read at the 2016 MassPoetry Festival presentation of *Poets at the Bar: Five Practicing Massachusetts Attorneys Who Are Published Poets*. He is listed in the *Poets & Writers'* Directory of Poets and Writers; is one of three MassPoetry representatives for Bristol County, Massachusetts; and is the founder of the Poetry as Verdict project providing a public venue for high school student-poets to read their work. Since 1995, in non-pandemic times, he resides part of the year on the Greek island Hydra.

His author's web site is *www.johnlholgerson.com*.

www.ingramcontent.com/pod-product-compliance
Lightning Source LLC
Chambersburg PA
CBHW020330010526
44107CB00054B/2049